TATIANA SIBIRSKAYA

A LIFE DEVOTED TO PERFORMING
GOD'S MIRACLES

Carolyn Fryer

ISBN 978-1-68197-272-5 (Paperback)
ISBN 978-1-68197-553-5 (Hard Cover)
ISBN 978-1-68197-554-2 (Digital)

Copyright © 2016 by Carolyn Fryer
All rights reserved. No part of this publication may be reproduced, distributed, or transmitted in any form or by any means, including photocopying, recording, or other electronic or mechanical methods without the prior written permission of the publisher. For permission requests, solicit the publisher via the address below.

Christian Faith Publishing, Inc.
296 Chestnut Street
Meadville, PA 16335
www.christianfaithpublishing.com

Printed in the United States of America

CONTENTS

Preface 5
Foreword 7
Childhood 9
The Death of Tatiana's Mother 17
God Opens Tatiana's Vision 18
Confirmation 21
Tatiana Moves to America 27
A Miraculous Return to Life 33
San Francisco 35
Return to Brooklyn 38
September 11, 2001 41
God versus Evil 43
More Miracles 45
Testimonials 48
Questions and Answers 62
Bibliography 67

PREFACE

Having known Tatiana Sibirskaya as a healer for over twenty years, I can say from personal experience that Tatiana has truly been given the gift of healing, serving as a conduit for God's energy to share with those who seek her help. Devoted to God her entire life, Tatiana is a selfless individual who prays for millions of people every day. She calls herself one of God's soldiers, and doing God's work is her life mission.

The first time I met Tatiana, I was holding my one-year-old in my arms, and she gasped, asking what had happened to his head six months earlier. He had fallen, hit his head and ended up with a concussion, but there were no longer any visible physical signs of the injury. The only way she could have known about the injury was to somehow "see" it herself. She assured me that she would pray for him, and he would be fine…and he was. Since that time, my family and I have received God's healing energy through Tatiana more times than I could possibly count. With the help of God, she has healed us from life-threatening illnesses, serious injuries, and emotional traumas. She has also healed many of our friends, along with millions of people around the world. The purpose of this book is to tell her story, share testimonies from her clients, and spread the word of God's miracles on earth. According to Tatiana, all one needs is an open mind and a desire to be healed, as Tatiana uses God's healing energy to do the rest.

"A person should believe in God, in Eternal Good, in miracles," says Tatiana. "Faith is one of the ways to the cure. No doctor can help a patient who refuses to fight for his own life. If there is no faith, there should at least be hope."[1]

In 2004, Tatiana wrote a brief autobiography, *Autobiography of a Faith Healer*, which was the starting point for this book. As a result of our ongoing friendship, Tatiana asked me to write a more complete history about her life's work incorporating text from her second writing *Miracles and Mysteries of God*, articles, photographs, testimonials, and material from our personal discussions in an effort to educate, spread word of God's miracles, and bring hope to people who in desperation feel that they have nowhere to turn. In Tatiana's words, "With God, anything is possible. All you have to do is ask, and be open to being healed. We work…"

---

1. Hurgin, Boris, *Bow to Tatiana with Gratitude*, "Novoye Russkoe Slovo," "New Russian Word," April 19, 1994, 1.

FOREWORD

I never intended to write about myself. My work spoke for itself, and my patients carried my story to others so that they may benefit too. One evening, I finished work late, as I often do. After a long day, I always try to relax by listening to music. I also love to watch interesting movies and read motivating books. I love autobiographical books about great individuals, and also spiritual books, and books about philosophy, poetry, and art.

Suddenly, at 2:30 a.m. on July 16, 2004, I heard the voice of Mary. She said to me, "You must

Tatiana Sibirskaya

write about your life. People are waiting." I answered her, "I don't even know where to begin. I never wrote." She replied in a soft voice, "The book is already written." And immediately I saw the text, took a pen, and quickly began to write. My entire life flashed in front of me, from early childhood to the present time. I not only heard and saw myself, but I relived it all over again. Mary, Mother of God, reminded me and showed me my entire life so that I could write this autobiography.[2]

I thought that I will not write anymore after my "special" biography, where I couldn't add anything by myself. I only heard and wrote and relived wonderful periods of my life, dictated and shown to me by Mary. However on Friday, June 29, 2005, at 3:00 a.m., I heard again the voice of Mary, "You must write all of this. People must know about it," and I saw the text for *Miracles and Mysteries of God*.[3]

---

2. Sibirskaya, Tatiana, *Autobiography of a Faith Healer*, 2004.
3. Sibirskaya, Tatiana, *Miracles and Mysteries of God*, 2005.

CHILDHOOD

The youngest of three children, Tatiana Sibirskaya was born in Orenburg in the very picturesque area of South Ural, Russia. She was the daughter of a soldier who fought through World War II, only to become an invalid and be pensioned off.[4] Although her parents, Ilya and Maria, were deeply religious (Russian Orthodox), they never talked about religion for fear of persecution by the Russian government. Undeterred, Tatiana learned about God and the power of prayer from her mother's much older sister, whom she called grandmother, and maintained a deeply rooted faith from a very young age.

Tatiana recalled, "Despite atheistic propaganda in the Soviet schools, I deeply believed in God and knew that only He can help troubled people."[5] She was never afraid to follow her devotion to God, despite a Soviet antitheistic government that prohibited practicing religion. Her

Tatiana at the age of two

---

4. Gris, Henry, *And So Tatiana Sibirskaya Became the World's Latest Healer*, International Artists Guild, Ltd. Matthew, Inc., Nov.17, 1992, 1.
5. Sibirskaya, Tatiana, *Autobiography of a Faith Healer*, 2004, 1.

deeply felt love of God inspired her to go to church every Sunday, sneaking into the few open churches to ask for God's blessings.

She said, "In my childhood and now, I love going to church. We didn't have a church in our village so my grandmother rode into town. With tears I implored her to take me too, and she couldn't refuse. The beautiful icons, burning candles, and church chorus made a big impression on me. I felt how my feet raised from the floor, and I was flying and mingling among many angels."[6]

"Grandmother Claudia was my mother's older sister, and we tenderly called her grandmother. I loved to spend time with her. She was very interesting. She had a big house and big garden, and huge maples grew in this garden alongside berries and fruits. There were several beehives, which produced honey. In the evening, grandmother took from her beautiful cabinet a Bible, covered in a thin, silver binding and read it aloud. She explained parts of the text to me, the meaning of which I didn't understand at that time. When she read the Bible, she stood in front of the icons. Grandmother had many icons in her house. Usually she lit candles and on religious holidays, she also lit an icon-lamp. Somehow she was able to save all these things. Grandmother's house was like a temple. There was tranquility and quietness and during her Bible reading I saw angels and many holy people emanating radiance. Mary also appeared. In my parent's house we didn't have many icons and there was no Bible."[7]

Tatiana at the age of eight

Growing up surrounded by the beauty of the Ural Mountains, Tatiana often sought refuge by a favorite stream in the peace and quiet of the woods. She found that being close to nature relaxed her and renewed her energy.[8] As a young child, she would dis-

---

6. Sibirskaya, Tatiana, *Autobiography of a Faith Healer*, 2004, 5.
7. Sibirskaya, Tatiana, *Autobiography of a Faith Healer*, 2004, 6.
8. Tatiana Sibirskaya in discussion with the author, December, 2015.

appear for hours while communing with nature's animals, trees, and streams, never fearing the wild animals that lurked in the woods because she knew that God would protect her. Ailing friends and neighbors often noticed that they felt better in her presence, along with the many wild animals that were attracted to her. "I loved the Ural Mountains, I went far from home, deep into the mountains regardless of the season. There I collected precious and semi-precious stones. I didn't take any food or water with me. At the foothills of the mountains were springs with delicious cold water. I drank this water with joy, collecting it in my palms. Nature provided me with wild berries, wood nuts, and wild cucumbers for food. Many wild boars lived in the mountains, but they did not touch me. Apparently they sensed my kindness toward them. In winter, I went skiing. Once I saw a herd of elk running toward me with great speed. I thought they would stampede me, but they went around me peacefully and sniffed me. Suddenly they calmed down and turned back into the forest."[9] One day while she was skiing, suddenly two airplane seats crashed right next to her, but she had heard no explosion. Soon afterward, two pilots came to her and asked if she knew of a repair shop. She told them where they could find one but suddenly noticed that they didn't have any bruises or injuries from the crash. According to her, "It was a miracle. God helped these men."[10]

Tatiana's parents never worried about her because she was very responsible and they knew that she was special. She reminisced, "My parents were kind and pious people. They never had any worries about me.[11] I grew up as an independent and calm girl. I remember myself since I was 10 years old. In childhood everyone called me 'little grandma' because they liked me and felt very comfortable with grandma. I was different from my sister and brother, they were like the other children."[12] Tatiana soon realized that she had a special gift and treasured the solitary days meditating and praying in the Ural Mountains.

---

9. Sibirskaya, Tatiana, *Autobiography of a Faith Healer*, 2004, 3.
10. Sibirskaya, Tatiana, *Autobiography of a Faith Healer*, 2004, 4.
11. Sibirskaya, Tatiana, *Autobiography of a Faith Healer*, 2004, 2.
12. Grant, Alexander, *Tatiana Sibirskaya—the Messenger of God's Will*, "Novoye Russkoe Slovo," "New Russian Word," April 4, 1997, 2.

TATIANA SIBIRSKAYA: A LIFE DEVOTED TO PERFORMING GOD'S MIRACLES

One day in the Ural Mountains, the Virgin Mary appeared to her and started to prepare her for a life devoted to doing God's work. Tatiana was awestruck by her beautiful shining face, her gorgeous hair, her twice woven braids, and her delicate hands. "I wanted to share this with my mother. I wanted to tell her that kind, tender Mary came to me in her shining light and that I felt good in her presence. I opened my mouth to try to tell her, but no sound came out."[13] Although Tatiana was still a very young girl, God prepared her for a life mission of healing by showing her in dreams about good and evil, and educating her about everything: demons, witches, helping people, and giving her knowledge.[14] God sealed her lips so she couldn't tell anyone. "This became my protection until I was thirty-five. I kept silent always. I could not share this with anyone, not even my parents, or my brother and sister. Heaven protected me, prepared me, and taught me how to serve people. In the former Soviet Union I would have been destroyed."[15]

This caused her great distress because she couldn't discuss the one thing that mattered most to her—her closeness to God and the Virgin Mary. Feeling burdened with her secret, she felt isolated and retreated to the woods, consoling herself with prayer. "I felt no interest with my peers. They mostly irritated me with their behavior and interests. Often I secluded myself and tried to find peace in nature. Not far from our house ran a little river. I loved this river. I talked to it and the river responded to me. It was a mountain river and was very cold. Its wave rose up and touched my lips and I was glad that the river loved me. It turned warm for me. On both sides of the river grew many trees, and beautiful flowers. I talked to the flowers and trees, and they responded to me with love. I saw how flowers were attracted to me."[16]

During Tatiana's excursions into the forest, the visions of Mary would often appear. "In silence and solitude Mary came to me. To see

---

13. Sibirskaya, Tatiana, *Autobiography of a Faith Healer*, 2004, 2.
14. Tatiana Sibirskaya in discussion with the author, December, 2015.
15. Sibirskaya, Tatiana, *Autobiography of a Faith Healer*, 2004, 2–3.
16. Sibirskaya, Tatiana, *Autobiography of a Faith Healer*, 2004, 3.

her I tried to seclude myself more often. My parents saw that I was not an ordinary child, but they never asked me about anything; they simply observed me."[17] Tatiana felt totally shielded from harm until one day when she was running barefoot in the woods after a warm summer rain when a sliver from a broken milk bottle badly cut her foot. "After a warm summer rain, I loved to run barefoot. One day, a big sliver from a milk bottle plunged deep into my heel. My legs were dirty and the blood poured from the wound, but I didn't feel pain. I took out this sliver and the blood stopped. The wound suddenly was healed, and there was so sign of an injury. Another day I went fishing with my father. He unintentionally ripped my skin under the eye with his fishing pole. Again, blood poured from the wound. My father was very scared, but suddenly everything was healed. I never had to fear. I was confident that Heaven would help me."[18] After experiencing several other healings from childhood accidents, Tatiana was completely assured that her deep faith and trust in God protected her from harm. "I loved riding the bicycle, and one day, descending from the mountain road, I felt that my brakes weren't working properly. I saw a big truck coming my way, and to avoid a collision, I threw my body on the side of the road. As a result, I ripped my stomach so that even my inner parts were visible. I wasn't scared for myself, but I was scared how my mother would be upset when she would see me in this condition. As I thought about this, everything was suddenly healed. There wasn't even any scar left. I sat back on my bicycle and rode home. And such healing began to come to all my relatives, and to all for whom I prayed. I prayed to Heaven for them when they were ill, and they were healed. When I was growing up I came to understand that this was the work of God, and all saints, angels and archangels. I learned that they give instant healing to those with a deep faith."[19]

---

17. Sibirskaya, Tatiana, *Autobiography of a Faith Healer*, 2004, 4.
18. Sibirskaya, Tatiana, *Autobiography of a Faith Healer*, 2004, 4.
19. Sibirskaya, Tatiana, *Autobiography of a Faith Healer*, 2004, 5.

TATIANA SIBIRSKAYA: A LIFE DEVOTED TO PERFORMING GOD'S MIRACLES

As a young girl, Tatiana was always helping people in need. "I was very compassionate to everyone, especially to those who suffered and to those who were deprived. Since childhood I felt in me power that I could help unfortunate people. Though I was little, I always was around sick old people and little children, and I soon noticed that they began to feel good just by being in my presence. I helped old people in any way I could; I cleaned their house, shoveled snow, brought them water from the well, and did their shopping. Mary, Mother of God, helped me to do all these things."[20] Cleaning houses enabled her to earn money so she could buy or make food for starving people. She also knew how to sew and would make clothes for people who were cold and couldn't afford them. Although people were attracted to her because they felt good in her presence, she was quite lonely because no one truly understood her, not even her siblings or her parents. She read many books about God and was an excellent student because God gave her all the knowledge she needed. "I was getting good grades in school. My knowledge was deeper than my earthly teachers gave me. Heaven gave me higher knowledge and some teachers became irritated by it, as well as my classmates."[21] "In school I tried to maintain relationships with my classmates. I had many activities, such as acrobatics, sewing, needlework, woodcraft, and various sport activities. It was very easy for me. I felt the help of God in everything I did."[22] Although she started to attend technical college in Almetevsk, her teachers soon recognized that there was

Tatiana at the age of sixteen

---

20. Sibirskaya, Tatiana, *Autobiography of a Faith Healer*, 2004, 2.
21. Sibirskaya, Tatiana, *Autobiography of a Faith Healer*, 2004, 4.
22. Sibirskaya, Tatiana, *Autobiography of a Faith Healer*, 2004, 5.

nothing new that they could teach her. "I finished High School and was considering what to do next. I decided to go to the city of Almetevsk to study and pursue a profession, but after only six months I went back home. I was a good student at school, though there were some difficulties: sometimes I told the material of the textbook by heart without any efforts, teachers did not like that at all."[23]

Tatiana at the age of twenty-one

"I worked a little as a bookkeeper in the management of a collective farm. Then I went to the city of Tomsk in Siberia to pursue a higher education. But once again there were obstacles and conflicts with university professors. They envied the extensive knowledge that God gave me. Apparently it wasn't my destiny to get a university diploma."[24]

After giving up on any thought of pursuing a college education, Tatiana got a job as a radio technician at a factory, managing thirty employees working under her. Earning a good salary, every weekend she would cook food to share with her employees.

---

23. Grant, Alexander, *Tatiana Sibirskaya—the Messenger of God's Will*, "Novoye Russkoe Slovo," "New Russian Word," April 4, 1997, 2.
24. Sibirskaya, Tatiana, *Autobiography of a Faith Healer*, 2004, 6–7.

THE DEATH OF TATIANA'S MOTHER

"The first time Heaven showed to me when a soul leaves the body was when my mother was dying on January 19, 1984 at 11:20 a.m. I saw her in another body with Light, two angels at her sides. That other body touched my left cheek as if to say farewell to me. To follow mother's will, I didn't ask Heaven to prolong her life. My mother was spiritual and she understood that with God is better than on Earth. All of us here on Earth learn, and when we are ready, we go to God and don't come back on Earth anymore."[25]

"Mother didn't know about my wonderful gift, only felt that she was always calm in my presence, aches went away."[26]

---

25. Sibirskaya, Tatiana, *Miracles and Mysteries of God*, 2005, 2.
26. Sibirskaya, Tatiana, *Miracles and Mysteries of God*, 2005, 2.

GOD OPENS TATIANA'S VISION

When Tatiana was thirty-five years old, God "opened her vision" so she could see people's organs, blood vessels, etc. This would enable her to see everything down to the smallest capillaries (as if viewing X-rays, MRI scans, and CAT scans), enabling her to accurately diagnose illnesses.

Tatiana recollected, "My life was not any different from lives of other Soviet people: work, family. But one day I felt very sick: terrible headaches, heartaches."[27] Her entire body ached. She had a high fever, suffered from nausea and lay listless in her bed. She was taken to the local hospital where she thought they could take care of her, but they didn't recognize the symptoms.[28] "After a series of examinations and tests the diagnosis was healthy. So I left the hospital, though the symptoms persisted."[29] The next day, when her husband came home from work, he turned on the dim light in their hall while

---

27. Viktorova, L., *I See Your Heart*, "Vecherniy Dushanbe," "Evening Dushanbe," October 2, 1991, 1.
28. Gris, Henry, *And So Tatiana Sibirskaya Became the World's Latest Healer*, International Artists Guild, Ltd. Matthew, Inc., Nov.17, 1992, 2-3.
29. Viktorova, L., *I See Your Heart*, "Vecherniy Dushanbe," "Evening Dushanbe," October 2, 1991, 1.

still bundled in his heavy overcoat when she caught sight of him. "I looked at my husband and couldn't understand what was going on: I saw all his organs—lungs, stomach, liver, intestines. I felt dizzy."[30] In shock, she fainted. Scared, and unable to explain, she didn't tell her husband until much later. She stayed indoors, seeing no one and gradually calmed down enough to figure out what to do.[31] "When I touched my son's shoulder, he screamed that it burnt him. Later, I saw a red mark on his shoulder where I put my hand."[32] Suddenly, when going to work by bus every day, Tatiana couldn't help noticing the pathological issues of people around her: "This man has a hernia, and that blond has problems with her left lung…"[33] The burden of this suddenly acquired knowledge was hard. "When I addressed the doctors with this problem, they got interested in me, the news came to Moscow."[34] "Up until thirty-five I could ask God to heal sick people with my strong faith, but I couldn't see their problems of their organs. At thirty-five I began to see these things for the first time. I could also begin to tell people of my miraculous visions with holy people, the angels and Mary."[35]

"After I discovered this ability in me to see inside the human body, all my problems disappeared but at the same time I felt almost a physical necessity to be with people. When I was at home alone I felt as if somebody was pushing me: go and help people."[36] Initially, she had a hard time adjusting to her newfound visual abilities and

---

30. Viktorova, L., *I See Your Heart*, "Vecherniy Dushanbe," "Evening Dushanbe," October 2, 1991, 1.
31. Gris, Henry, *And So Tatiana Sibirskaya Became the World's Latest Healer*, International Artists Guild, Ltd. Matthew, Inc., Nov.17, 1992, 3.
32. Viktorova, L., *I See Your Heart*, "Vecherniy Dushanbe," "Evening Dushanbe," October 2, 1991, 1.
33. Lishak, Arnold, *I Am Happy to Bring Happiness to People*, Interview with Tatiana Sibirskaya, "Mir," October 2-8, 1992, 3.
34. Viktorova, L., *I See Your Heart*, "Vecherniy Dushanbe," "Evening Dushanbe," October 2, 1991, 1.
35. Sibirskaya, Tatiana, *Autobiography of a Faith Healer*, 2004, 7.
36. Viktorova, L., *I See Your Heart*, "Vecherniy Dushanbe," "Evening Dushanbe," October 2, 1991, 1.

wasn't able to eat. She lost a lot of weight, becoming very skinny but eventually learned to cope with God's new gift.

When she left her factory work after seventeen years of employment there to do God's work, most of her coworkers cried and begged her not to leave. "Heaven forced me to quit my job at the factory and completely dedicate my life to people. Even though I worked there for seventeen years and earned a decent wage, I quit my job without any doubt and fear. I was thinking clearly, since God called on me to serve people, He will help me in everything."[37]

---

37. Sibirskaya, Tatiana, *Autobiography of a Faith Healer*, 2004, 7.

CONFIRMATION

Word spread about Tatiana's remarkable abilities, and doctors all around got interested in her phenomenon. She soon found herself among prestigious circles of professionals, which she never embraced. It was not her way to mingle with the rich and famous, since her life was devoted to helping the sick, deprived, and poor. "I was never attracted to idle earthly fame. Most important for me has always been, in the name of God, serving people in God's glory. I'm very grateful to Heaven for this wonderful gift."[38]

When medical specialists in Tomsk (Tatiana's home city, and a large industrial city in the vast, freezing expanse of Siberia) heard about her extraordinary abilities, she was sent to leading research centers for confirmation. "In January 1991, I was living in Moscow. I was invited to the Medical Academy for approbation of my healing abilities. I explained to the professors that there was no need to examine my brain; this gift was a gift from God. I was born with it. Thank God! They understood me and stopped probing for a more earthly explanation. They brought me to their seriously ill relatives and friends. I diagnosed and healed them with the help of God and all the saints. Miraculous recovery happened. My approbation was successful. From January to June many people were healed."[39] After the confirma-

---

38. Sibirskaya, Tatiana, *Autobiography of a Faith Healer*, 2004, 9.
39. Sibirskaya, Tatiana, *Autobiography of a Faith Healer*, 2004, 9-10.

tion results achieved by clinical tests proved to be absolutely correct, Tatiana was asked to work with patients in the urological department of the Moscow First Medical Institute, named after Sechenov.[40] She worked in the research group of world renowned medical scientist and academician, R. I. Bagramov, who certified 100 percent reliability of Tatiana's diagnosis, when even qualified specialists with the most modern equipment were not sure about the patient's condition.[41] Tatiana never made a mistake. She diagnosed illnesses and treated several patients, curing them. "That was my first big victory: I showed that I not only could diagnose people but also cure them."[42] "People began to invite me to hospitals to help seriously ill patients."[43]

(In the interest of confidentiality, all names of the patients have been changed):

> Stave, 11 months old, had testicle dropsy. Doctors were going to operate. It was gone during my first session with him.
> Irina, 12 years old, had burst appendicitis. Pus spread all over her abdominal cavity. Everything was gone after five sessions with me, without surgery.
> Kostya, 13 years old, had cerebral palsy. After ten sessions the muscles of his arms and legs straightened out. His leg was shorter than the other, but it too straightened out.
> Galina, 46 years old, suffered from asthma for a long time. After ten sessions the asthma was gone.
> Oleg, 26 years old, had a brain tumor, and required trepanation of the skull. After ten sessions, the tumor was gone.
> Faina, 43 years old, was diagnosed with stomach cancer. After ten sessions, she was healthy.

---

40. Gris, Henry, *And So Tatiana Sibirskaya Became the World's Latest Healer*, International Artists Guild, Ltd. Matthew, Inc., Nov.17, 1992, 2.
41. Hurgin, Boris, *Bow to Tatiana with Gratitude*, "Novoye Russkoe Slovo," "New Russian Word," April 19, 1994, 2.
42 Lishak, Arnold, *I Am Happy to Bring Happiness to People*, Interview with Tatiana Sibirskaya, "Mir," October 2–8, 1992, 1.
43 Sibirskaya, Tatiana, *Autobiography of a Faith Healer*, 2004, 8.

Many other miraculous recoveries also occurred during this period...[44]

"How happy I was when human beings on the verge of death opened their eyes. Infants, who could not yet speak words of gratitude when I healed serious illness, just looked at me and smiled. I cried with happiness as people recovered. I saw how powerful energy from God directly entered all cells, bones, muscles and organs of the patients, and cleaned him or her physically and spiritually. I explained to people that God was the healer, not I. I explained that I asked God, Mary, Jesus Christ, all the saints, angels, and archangels with prayers of deep faith, sometimes on my knees with tears to help sick people. Deep faith from the patient also has forceful power for healing."[45]

One night after she had been working late at the hospital, Tatiana left to go home, but couldn't get there because the buses had stopped running for the night. "To go to my house was possible by foot, through the forest; it was only a few minutes' walk. But it was already night time and the forest was dark and scary. I just stood near the hospital not sure what to do. Jesus Christ came to me, gave me his hand and said, "Do not be afraid, I'm with you." He led me safely home through the forest."[46] This was her first encounter with Jesus Christ.

Tatiana put in two years working in Moscow, where she never lost a patient but helped hundreds.[47] Working in hospitals gave her a substantial amount of medical training,[48] helping her to communicate more effectively with her clients. She also read special medical literature to help her diagnose patients,[49] who began to come from all

---

44. Sibirskaya, Tatiana, *Autobiography of a Faith Healer*, 2004, 10.
45. Sibirskaya, Tatiana, *Autobiography of a Faith Healer*, 2004, 8.
46. Sibirskaya, Tatiana, *Autobiography of a Faith Healer*, 2004, 9.
47. Gris, Henry, *And So Tatiana Sibirskaya Became the World's Latest Healer*, International Artists Guild, Ltd. Matthew, Inc., Nov.17, 1992, 5.
48. Basin, Yuri, *Ordinary Miracle*, "Yevreiski Mir," Jewish World, May 2, 1997 #4, 2.
49. Lishak, Arnold, *I Am Happy to Bring Happiness to People*, Interview with Tatiana Sibirskaya, "Mir," October 2–8, 1992, 1.

over the world to be treated by Tatiana. They came from the former Soviet Union, Western Europe, and Israel.[50]

When given the ability to "see" people, Tatiana also gained powerful healing energy in her hands. From this time onward, she absorbed clients' negative energy, relieving them of their suffering over a series of visits. It became necessary for her to wash her hands in between clients to dispel the negative energy absorbed from each person. She had to be very careful not to absorb her patients' pains and diseases.[51] God told her to always have a burning candle on the table when she received patients in order to protect herself so that all evil would burn in the flame of the candle.[52] When receiving patients, Tatiana lights a candle, explaining that all evil and disease are burned in a holy flame.[53] She tells her clients that God cures them, and the stronger a client's faith, the sooner the cure comes. Working with holy water and paper towels, Tatiana explains that they will all be filled with God's healing energy. She also asks her clients to take off their watches.[54] The healing energy from God radiates through her to the client, often interfering with electrical

Tatiana uses a lit candle to help dispel evil and disease

---

50. Basin, Yuri, *Ordinary Miracle*, "Yevreiski Mir," Jewish World, May 2, 1997 #4, 2.
51. Lishak, Arnold, *I Am Happy to Bring Happiness to People*, Interview with Tatiana Sibirskaya, "Mir," October 2–8, 1992, 4.
52. Lishak, Arnold, *I Am Happy to Bring Happiness to People*, Interview with Tatiana Sibirskaya, "Mir," October 2–8, 1992, 4.
53. Basin, Yuri, *Ordinary Miracle*, "Yevreiski Mir," Jewish World, May 2, 1997 #4, 1.
54. Viktorova, L., *I See Your Heart*, "Vecherniy Dushanbe," "Evening Dushanbe," October 2, 1991, 2.

currents. Tatiana has caused the premature demise of several refrigerators, watches, clock radios, cordless phones, cell phones, stereos, microwaves, and computers as the energy from her hands causes a surge that destroys electronics. Now she changes cordless phones between patients so they don't get too hot.[55]

"My older sister lives in Tomsk, Siberia, and when we speak with each other on the phone, I say to her, 'Now I will hug you, only please don't be afraid.' After a while she says to me, 'Take your hands off my shoulders. I feel heat.'"[56] Tatiana never touches patients with her hands due to their strong concentration of energy.

According to Tatiana, "If I tell you how it is happening you would not believe me. It sounds like impossible. Well…I concentrate and I can see through a man. I study organs carefully. If I am not quite sure about something I feel like somebody is helping…I see healthy and diseased organs in different colors…I treat with my eyes when I direct the energy into the affected organ. I am just a transformer of the healing energy."[57]

According to her, God and the Apostles appear in the "videocenter" of her consciousness, concentrating their power and energy on her, as she "transforms" this energy for diagnosing and curing her patients.[58] "I see Christ, Saints, Angels…before I got this gift I did not study the Holy Bible carefully. And then I saw the light, recognized the images of Saints. They help me to cure people. Now human pain and suffering is my pain and suffering."[59] "I work hard, sometimes without any rest, because I want to help people, to bring them good."[60] "I absorb their problems in my body. Sometimes I have no strength left at

---

55. Tatiana Sibirskaya in discussion with the author, December, 2015.
56. Sibirskaya, Tatiana, *Autobiography of a Faith Healer*, 2004, 18–19.
57. Viktorova, L., *I See Your Heart*, "Vecherniy Dushanbe," "Evening Dushanbe," October 2, 1991, 2.
58. Lishak, Arnold, *I Am Happy to Bring Happiness to People*, Interview with Tatiana Sibirskaya, "Mir," October 2–8, 1992.
59. Viktorova, L., *I See Your Heart*, "Vecherniy Dushanbe," "Evening Dushanbe," October 2, 1991, 2.
60. Viktorova, L., *I See Your Heart*, "Vecherniy Dushanbe," "Evening Dushanbe," October 2, 1991, 2.

all. When I have time, I fall into a deep sleep, and then God, Mary and all the saints heal me, giving me renewed strength. Sometimes, when I'm healed, I am still out of my body and in spirit, together with Mary I continue to help people on earth. Once, Mary treated me to an apple. Never in my life did I eat such an apple. It was really a 'heavenly' apple. But time passed and Heaven brought me back into my body. Yes, this is a miracle. I can be in both worlds, higher and earthly, at the same time. The higher is a spiritual world. The spiritual world brings peace, tranquility and love to earth. One God. One Heaven for all religions, for all people. I love all people, I believe in One God, and I respect all religions. The path to God is one—love. With deep faith it is easy to overcome difficulties of any kind and change life for a better way. It is important to strive for spiritual growth.

Although Tatiana is grateful for her gifts, her life is far from easy. "There is a big difference between Paradise and life. In Paradise there is no pain or illness and everything is beautiful. When I go there, I don't want to leave, but God throws me back to my earthly body and I cry because I don't want to come back and feel all of that pain and suffering."[61]

In early 1991, Tatiana was visiting a spa near Sochi on the Black Sea, when she met with a Russian American who had been eager to meet her. Stunned by her ability to cure people, he insisted that she come to America. She was needed there, and he would help get her there. Tatiana sought an answer in prayer. Should she go? She got the message: go.[62] She was shown a vision of the United States. "I saw Manhattan and all its skyscrapers, and I walked on the streets of this wondrous city. During these times people in Russia knew little about the United States, but for me, Heaven showed me this country beforehand. Two months had passed since that vision, after which I went to the U.S.A."[63]

---

61. Tatiana Sibirskaya in discussion with the author, December, 2015.
62. Gris, Henry, *And So Tatiana Sibirskaya Became the World's Latest Healer*, International Artists Guild, Ltd. Matthew, Inc., Nov.17, 1992, 5–6.
63. Sibirskaya, Tatiana, *Autobiography of a Faith Healer*, 2004, 11.

TATIANA MOVES TO AMERICA

After applying for an exit visa which was granted much faster than expected, Tatiana moved to the United States in June, 1991, where she could practice religion without persecution. She landed at Kennedy Airport (New York) at four o'clock in the morning. Arriving in a strange country where people spoke a different language, she was met by new friends who would take care of her. They brought her to Brooklyn, which overflowed with Russian émigrés, in a Moscow on the Hudson. Catching a glimpse of a Greek Orthodox Church, she knew she had found a new home.[64] "I stayed in New York, in the Borough of Brooklyn. I was there from June 21 to August 12, 1991. This country made a

Tatiana at Brighton Beach in Brooklyn

---

64. Gris, Henry, *And So Tatiana Sibirskaya Became the World's Latest Healer*, International Artists Guild, Ltd. Matthew, Inc., Nov.17, 1992, 6.

great impression on me with its strength, wealth and hospitality. My friends showed me the sights and acquainted me with the New York of my vision. I was in love with the Verrazano Bridge. I especially liked Manhattan, its museums (Metropolitan Museum in particular), the Metropolitan Opera and the Twin Towers of the World Trade Center. I was also impressed by the Statue of Liberty and Ellis Island. I began to ask God to send to this wonderful city pure and healthy energy. And now I constantly ask Heaven to bless all Americans with healthy energy in all fifty states."[65]

During this first visit to America, Tatiana was able to help many people:

> Mary suffered from thrombosis of the carotid artery, but because of her age, she wasn't able to undergo surgery. After ten sessions, her artery was clean.
> Tanya had a fibroma of the womb, but after ten visits the fibroma was gone.
> Leo was diagnosed with diabetes, but after ten sessions, the diabetes tormenting him for many years had suddenly stopped bothering him.
> Lenya had a gastric ulcer, but after ten sessions the ulcer was gone.[66]

Many other people were healed was well. Everything disappeared without a trace: kidney stones, benign and malignant tumors and cysts. "Pneumonia, leukemia, Parkinson's disease, Alzheimer's disease—everything went away because these patients had deep faith and no doubts."[67]

"After a short rest, I went to Dushanbe, the capital of Tadjikistan. I wanted to help more suffering people. Pain and human sorrow were now my pain and sorrow. I worked in Dushanbe for two weeks and tried to see as many people as possible. I worked for five days on a large audience in the Union Palace Hall. I asked of the people sitting

---

65. Sibirskaya, Tatiana, *Autobiography of a Faith Healer*, 2004, 11.
66. Sibirskaya, Tatiana, *Autobiography of a Faith Healer*, 2004, 12.
67. Sibirskaya, Tatiana, *Autobiography of a Faith Healer*, 2004, 12.

in the hall, who began to feel better or whose pain went away, to stand up and speak on the microphone:

> Gena, 14 years old, suffered with cerebral palsy, but after five sessions he left his crutches in the hall.
> Mischa had pneumonia, but after only five sessions the pneumonia was gone.
> Galya suffered with acute pain in the vertebra, but after five sessions the pain went away.

I also worked privately, and when I was free from work, I tried to see the sights of this beautiful city."[68]

"On the morning of October 21, 1991, I traveled on a motor ship from Larnak to Haifa. Far from the Mediterranean Sea opened the white stone panorama of Haifa. When I got there, I underwent customs procedures and went straight to Tel Aviv. This was the first time I was acquainted with Israel, with its sights. The Holy Land is unusually picturesque and expressive with its strong contrasts, arid deserts, cliffs and beautiful oases. The Wailing Wall, the Mosque of Omar, the Church of all Nations, the Holy Tomb of Christ—all sacred places for all humanity. Mostly I tried to see the holy places."[69] While sightseeing at one stop, Tatiana found that she had gotten separated from her tour group and couldn't find her way back to the tour bus where she had left her passport, along with all of her money and personal belongings. With Tatiana feeling totally helpless, again Jesus took her by the hand and led her back to the bus.[70] Tatiana later recalled, "It was impossible to stop [sightseeing], but sick people waited for me. They invited me to help them and I began to work:

> Olya suffered from fecal incontinence, and depression, but after ten sessions everything was gone.

---

68. Sibirskaya, Tatiana, *Autobiography of a Faith Healer*, 2004, 12–13.
69. Sibirskaya, Tatiana, *Autobiography of a Faith Healer*, 2004, 13.
70. Tatiana Sibirskaya in discussion with the author, December, 2015.

> Sasha had kidney disease and waited for a donor, but after ten sessions the disease was gone and the transplant no longer necessary.
> Joseph suffered cardiac arrhythmia, and emphysema of the lungs, but after ten sessions he was healed.
> Ludmila had painful stones in the gall bladder, and hypertension, but after only eight sessions, she was healthy.
> David suffered from prostate cancer and depression. After ten sessions, everything went away."[71]

After leaving Israel, Tatiana returned to the United States on November 21, 1991, where she resumed working with clients. By April 27, 1992, it was time to go back to Moscow. "My suitcases were packed and everything was ready to go, but suddenly at five o'clock in the morning, I clearly heard a voice. 'You must stay in America and from here serve people.' I was invited to many countries to help the people, but God helped me make a choice—United States of America."[72]

"To get to know this country and its people better, and to help more suffering people, I traveled to various states. I traveled between Brooklyn and Philadelphia for three months. During this time, I worked in Brooklyn until noon, and then at 2 p.m. I started work in Philadelphia, only to travel back to Brooklyn late in the evening. During my work in Philadelphia many people were healed. I will give you several cases:

> Alesha, 10 years old, had asthma, but after eight sessions the asthma was gone.
> Igor suffered a knee injury, but after eight sessions the pain was gone.
> Liza had an allergy and a gastric ulcer, but after ten sessions she felt better.
> Efim, suffered ischemic heart disease but after ten visits everything was gone.

---

71. Sibirskaya, Tatiana, *Autobiography of a Faith Healer*, 2004, 13–14.
72. Sibirskaya, Tatiana, *Autobiography of a Faith Healer*, 2004, 14.

Oleg had a cyst of the thyroid gland, but after ten visits the cyst disappeared."[73]

"One day I had dinner in a restaurant. It was Saturday evening and the restaurant was full of people. Suddenly, two armed men entered and told the people to lie face down on the floor. Everyone followed their orders. I didn't panic, was very calm and began to pray. Miraculously, these men became calm and left and didn't hurt anybody."[74]

Tatiana opened an office in Brooklyn where she accepted clients. Continuing to do God's work from her office, word spread about her work through expos, word of mouth, and interviews with her on television and radio appearances. Although she had never studied English, God helped her to speak effortlessly. News traveled quickly about her special gift from God. Shortly after her arrival in the United States, Tatiana's unique talent drew the attention of local doctors. She recalled that soon after she arrived, she was offered a job at the Memorial Sloan Kettering Cancer Center in New York City.

Tatiana at HGTV in New York

She said no at the time, preferring to work with immigrants from the Soviet Union who needed her help. Not knowing any English at first, she felt more comfortable working with them.[75]

Before she knew it, she was being sought after by famous musicians, lawyers, doctors, and hospitals, among countless others.

---

73. Sibirskaya, Tatiana, *Autobiography of a Faith Healer*, 2004, 15–16.
74. Sibirskaya, Tatiana, *Autobiography of a Faith Healer*, 2004, 15.
75. Grant, Alexander, *Tatiana Sibirskaya—the Messenger of God's Will*, "Novoye Russkoe Slovo," "New Russian Word," April 4, 1997, 2.

Hospitals were asking her to join their staffs, and it seemed everyone wanted ownership of her services. Requests would come from Boston, Philadelphia, Baltimore, and San Francisco, asking her to share her gifts with clients. On weekends, she would stay up all night cooking for people, sharing her food with friends, church congregations, and homeless people.

A MIRACULOUS RETURN TO LIFE

On Saturday, May 2, 1994, at 6:30 in the morning, Tatiana heard a ring at the door. She hadn't been to sleep yet because in the stillness of the night she loves to read. When she opened the door, she saw a former patient, Semen, standing there, wriggling with pain. (He had previously been healed from diabetes mellitus with God's help and the Saints.) "I see the cause of his pain —his mission on Earth is finished, contract with God is accomplished, even though he was only 49 years old."[76] He died on her doorstep. "On Earth we seek causes of death, but for God there are no causes. I began to cry, asking Heaven to bring him back to life. His body was cold, pupils didn't react, I pinched him, and even pricked his finger with a needle, but there was no blood. I saw him in another body and with Light, and I felt like I've been watched by him at the height of 2 meters. This mystery of God calmed me, I began to pray."[77] This continued until 3:00 p.m. when he opened his eyes. "First, what I asked him was whether he remembers what was happening to him. He answered that he doesn't remember, said that he is very tired and wants to sleep. From the floor he went to the sofa, where he slept

---

76. Sibirskaya, Tatiana, *Miracles and Mysteries of God*, 2005, 2.
77. Sibirskaya, Tatiana, *Miracles and Mysteries of God*, 2005, 2–3.

until 6 p.m. until his wife came and woke him up. He, leaving the house told her that he didn't feel well and he came to Tatiana for help."[78] The couple had a son who is now an adult, and to this day, they celebrate the date of his return to life at a restaurant with family and relatives.

In June, 1994, Tatiana and her son went to Manhattan Beach. She was standing up to her knees in water, when suddenly a wave, taller than her, grabbed her and carried her out into the ocean. It "carries me into the open ocean with mad speed, I can't even resist this mighty force. I see in front of me a bright light, Jesus Christ. My brain is still working, first what I thought about is how my patients come to the office on Monday and don't find me there, then I thought about my son, how he will fear that I'm absent a long time and where am I. He read a book during this time and didn't see all this. And at this moment something, I understood it was Heaven, throws me out of the ocean on the sand with such force that my body was aching for two weeks. Later I told my son everything that I lived through this day. Apparently my contract is not finished and I'm still needed on Earth."[79]

---

78. Sibirskaya, Tatiana, *Miracles and Mysteries of God*, 2005, 3.
79. Sibirskaya, Tatiana, *Miracles and Mysteries of God*, 2005, 3–4.

SAN FRANCISCO

In the fall of 1994, Tatiana made her first trip to San Francisco. "I was there for one month. I arrived late in the evening. The next day, I went to see the Pacific Ocean. I was drawn to it; I felt its strong energy at a distance. But all of a sudden, on the shore I saw a baby seal in agony with a ruptured stomach. I stopped near him and began to ask God to help this poor animal. And then, a miracle happened. Before my eyes his wound began to mend and he opened his eyes and looked at me with gratitude. God helps not only people, but also animals and plants. People come to me with their sick pets:

Tatiana could feel the strong energy of the Pacific Ocean

> A cat with lymph cancer was healed and lived a long life.
> A dog suffered with long time cough, but after several sessions the cough was gone.
> A cat had ringworm of the scalp, but after several sessions she was cured.

Sick plants also recover. For sick animals and plants, I ask God to bless water. Animals drink this water, and of course, plants have to be watered."[80]

Tatiana speaking to an audience in San Francisco

"With prayers it is possible to stop any disasters of nature. Burning forests, pouring heavy rains, blizzards, even earthquakes. I ask God to stop these torrents. During my first trip to San Francisco everybody expected a big earthquake. God heard my prayers and prevented this terrible disaster. God also answered my prayers and healed many sick people in San Francisco:

> Klara had a clogged carotid artery, but everything was healed without surgery.
> Maria suffered for many years from Parkinson's disease and moved with difficulty. After her last session, she and I danced, while her friends witnessed this miracle and cried.
> Boris tested HIV positive, but with God's help he got rid of this terrible ailment."[81]

Tatiana returned to San Francisco in January 1996. "Before my arrival there were heavy rains and a hurricane. In the park lay many trees, uprooted by the hurricane. All the trees—tattered by the strong winds—needed help. I asked God to help the trees and flowers, and later witnessed how they revived.

---

80. Sibirskaya, Tatiana, *Autobiography of a Faith Healer*, 2004, 16.
81. Sibirskaya, Tatiana, *Autobiography of a Faith Healer*, 2004, 17.

There were also many people healed during my second visit:

Anton had a big cyst on his left kidney. Its protrusion was visible. When he left my office, his wife, who was a doctor, could not believe her eyes. The cyst dissolved on the first session.

Lina had a big fibroma of the womb, suffered from anemia and depression, and was weakened with pain in the vertebra. With my prayers and her deep faith she became absolutely healthy.

Sveta suffered from glaucoma, and her vision became worse. With God's help and her deep faith she was cured."[82]

Nature relaxes Tatiana and renews her energy

---

82. Sibirskaya, Tatiana, *Autobiography of a Faith Healer*, 2004, 17–18.

RETURN TO BROOKLYN

After returning to Brooklyn from San Francisco the second time, Tatiana didn't go anywhere for a while. "People came to me from many states, but there were many who could not come, so I worked with them over the telephone. The distance does not matter if a person sincerely believes. I work over the phone with people from Russia, the Ukraine, Canada, France, Israel, Switzerland, Germany, Australia and Britain."[83]

One night, Tatiana was enjoying dinner at a local restaurant. "The restaurant was full of people and near me was a table for four. There sat four middle aged males. One of them rose from his seat, made one step and fell on the floor unconscious. I immediately saw the cause of his fall—his heart shrank, the blood stopped the circulation. I began to ask God to bring him back. I don't know why my swift reaction was to bring the man back, whom I didn't even know. Maybe his mission on earth is finished. The men who were with him were at a loss. They sprinkled his face with cold water and dragged him out on the street. I was sitting at my table. I didn't see anything or anybody, only me, this man and God. Finally I saw how his heart began to work again, so I rose from the table and went outside. I saw them, sitting on the grass outside the restaurant, and saw him smiling. I felt a relief. I didn't even ask his name. I simply stopped for a

---

83. Sibirskaya, Tatiana, *Autobiography of a Faith Healer*, 2004, 18.

minute in silence. He looked at me and said, "Thank you." I didn't want to draw attention to myself. This was God's miracle. And such cases were many."[84]

Another example of God working miracles through Tatiana happened while she was working from her office in Brooklyn. "A call came in from a 67 year-old woman with an apparent heart attack. Over the phone, I immediately saw infarct, which is a localized area of tissue in the heart that is dying or has been deprived of its blood supply due to an obstruction by embolism or thrombosis. I began to pray for her, and I called her back after two hours. She no longer felt any pain."[85] Later that evening, Tatiana felt an acute pain in her heart and began to see infarct. "I saw Jesus and Mary. I fell asleep but later woke up, pain free. Thank God! I always think first about my patients. I wonder how they are doing without me. But Heaven always takes care of me."[86] This became evident to her on several occasions when she got badly injured. One time, she was high up on a ladder cleaning windows in her apartment, when the ladder slid out from under her, severing her finger in the process, breaking her leg, and ultimately causing her to lose consciousness. When she came to, God had healed her. Miraculously, God reattached the finger, leaving no scar or sign of injury.[87] Another miracle happened after she had a bad reaction to antibiotics a dentist had given her. She felt dizzy and fell hard on the uneven sidewalk, breaking teeth and bones in her body. She was covered in blood, but God made her invisible to all around so that bystanders wouldn't seek medical help, which could have been detrimental to her. God healed her and she managed to walk to her office, although still in shock. She suffered for many days afterward but was thankful that again God had saved her.[88]

Having very adverse reactions to drugs and any unnatural substances, Tatiana needs to avoid "modern" medicine, using only

---

84. Sibirskaya, Tatiana, *Autobiography of a Faith Healer*, 2004, 20.
85. Sibirskaya, Tatiana, *Autobiography of a Faith Healer*, 2004, 21.
86. Sibirskaya, Tatiana, *Autobiography of a Faith Healer*, 2004, 21.
87. Tatiana Sibirskaya in discussion with the author, December, 2015.
88. Tatiana Sibirskaya in discussion with the author, December, 2015.

unprocessed, real food and plants as medicine. Remedies she has suggested for illness have included eating fresh raw garlic, drinking fresh squeezed lemon juice on an empty stomach, honey, homemade chicken soup, cranberries simmered (but not boiled) in water as a tea for vitamin C and drinking green or herbal teas. She also recommends homemade beef broth, plain Greek yogurt and cheese to strengthen bones, and unsweetened cherry juice to cleanse the blood. "An apple a day" and fresh organic green vegetables are also on the list, providing a multitude of nutrients for general health.[89]

---

89. Tatiana Sibirskaya in discussion with the author, December, 2015.

SEPTEMBER 11, 2001

On September 11, 2001, everything changed. "We all remember this. It was a nice morning, with a blue sky and bright sunshine. Like many people, I turned on the TV that morning to find that all the channels showed the Twin Towers of the World Trade Center burning. This was a terrible tragedy not only for America, but for the world. I didn't go to my office. I canceled all appointments with my patients, and began to pray. I asked God to calm people who were in panic, to relieve pain to those who were burned and wounded. The collapse of the Twin Towers strongly shook the foundation of the earth. I was asking Heaven to calm the earth, and everything around it."[90] There was too much suffering in the world, and God told her to put an end to her social life and to work for the suffering people in the world. The energy around the world had become dark and evil, and there was much work to do. Every day she prays, asking God to clean the air of all evil and darkness, and to heal the planet.[91]

"On October 3, 2001, my son went to work on Ground Zero, to clean asbestos from nearby buildings. He worked there for three weeks and like me and all the others, was shocked by this cowardly and inhuman act of terrorists that took place on September 11,

---

90. Sibirskaya, Tatiana, *Autobiography of a Faith Healer*, 2004, 19.
91. Tatiana Sibirskaya in discussion with the author, December, 2015.

2001. All this time that he worked there, when he was falling asleep, he screamed loudly, his temperature was high, he cursed terrorists in his sleep. I sat nights near his bed, prayed to Heaven to send him peace and health. Though he is with spirit, he lived through this tragedy every night, and early every morning he went there to clean asbestos. I was afraid to lose my only child. Thank God! God and Heaven helped him."[92]

"First two years after this tragedy, when driving near this place I relived everything with my spirit: screams of the people, their moaning, and the oscillation of the earth around it. I prayed, asked God to calm souls of murdered, to calm the earth. Thank God! Now everything is quiet."[93]

"Now I ask Heaven every day to teach people not to kill each other, to prevent tragedies in the whole world, to make people healthy and happy. We are all God's children and in our interrelations must be forgiveness and love. The meaning of life does not lie in killing or destruction but in trying to find the road to God."[94]

"The covering of the Earth is brittle and thin, it will not sustain harm that people inflict on it. I pray during the day several times, to ask Heaven to protect planet Earth, and to change the mentality of people. No one is higher than our Creator, He can do anything, all is in His hands!!!"[95]

---

92. Sibirskaya, Tatiana, *Miracles and Mysteries of God*, 2005, 4.
93. Sibirskaya, Tatiana, *Miracles and Mysteries of God*, 2005, 4.
94. Sibirskaya, Tatiana, *Autobiography of a Faith Healer*, 2004, 19–20.
95. Sibirskaya, Tatiana, *Miracles and Mysteries of God*, 2005, 7.

GOD VERSUS EVIL

While in the midst of discussions for this book, Mary again spoke to Tatiana, requesting that she spread the word about the constant struggle between good and evil that surrounds us. According to Tatiana, "The devil [Satan], demons, black magic and witches all exist. They are very real, and there is a big fight between the devil and God." Speaking out against heavy metal music, violent video games, horror films, and the like, she retorts, "Don't invite the devil."[96] These dark influences destroy people's lives, ruining relationships, careers, and creating life threatening illnesses. "God will always win," but it is necessary to ask for God's help, praying every day. She also advocates wearing a cross and using icons for protection.

Tatiana recommends using
icons for protection

---

96. Tatiana Sibirskaya in discussion with the author, December, 2015.

Tatiana's first experience with witchcraft was when she was living in Moscow. She was treating a twelve-year-old girl who had three male demons inside of her. The girl suffered terribly and was very skinny because she couldn't eat. After asking God for protection for herself, Tatiana prayed for her. While in a deep sleep, the girl shook uncontrollably with her arms and legs flailing furiously, as "terrible deep voices came out of her mouth." They said, "What are you doing?" "Stop!" "Don't touch her!" Continuing with her prayers, the girl threw up, and the demons left her. Exorcisms are part of Tatiana's work in the constant fight against evil. When a person is inhabited by demons the victim becomes emotionally dead, creating a vacant look in their eyes, and becoming zombie-like. Often this leads to suicide as the devil claims their souls. Tatiana reiterates that "only God can help."[97]

While writing this book, black magic tried to destroy the author. Although not sick at the time, a mild earache started which within just a few hours became totally debilitating, causing the entire left side of her face and neck to swell and deafening her. It progressed very quickly. Tatiana "looked" inside the ear and saw black energy. As Tatiana prayed, she said in awe, "Jesus has his hand on your ear. Do you feel anything?"

It felt warm, and crackling, popping noises were heard inside the ear as the congestion eased. "Mary is standing over you, protecting you. She looks beautiful with her golden hair." Golden? "Yes, but unlike any color I have ever seen before on Earth." A few minutes later, the author asked if Jesus was still there. "Yes, but he has taken his hand away. Its energy would burn you if it was there too long." After that she continued to pray for the next twenty-four hours, eliminating the pain, clearing up the ear, restoring the hearing and bringing God's light with its healing energy back into the house. God had performed another miracle through Tatiana's prayers.

---

97. Tatiana Sibirskaya in discussion with the author, December, 2015.

MORE MIRACLES

Although it is impossible to list all of them, following are some miraculous case studies of some of Tatiana's patients.

In September 2003, at 7:00 p.m. a former patient, Nina, called Tatiana and said that in Montreal, Canada, a neighbor of Nina's cousin (Elena) lay dying. She was only fifty-six years old and the only daughter of her elderly parents. Elena had a strong wish to live, along with her parents' strong wishes for her to be restored to health. "My pleas, prayers with tears to God, to all Heaven brought her back to life. I read for her a prayer called 'Song to Holy Mother of God' 150 times a day, every day."[98]

"April 2005, at 6 p.m. Maria called me about her son-in-law. While he was trimming the tree, he fell on the ground from a ladder. I saw him in another body, with Light. At the beginning he didn't want much to come back to life, he told me that he is very tired. He was only 35 years old. He had a young wife, and two little boys. The wife and mother-in-law asked to bring Oleg back to life. But his wife doubted that he will come back in full health. I asked her to think positively and everything will be fine. He also doubted that he will be in full health and this held his return too. Thank God! Everything went okay. Oleg came back in full health. His mission on Earth was

---

98. Sibirskaya, Tatiana, *Miracles and Mysteries of God*, 2005, 4–5.

finished, but ardent pleas of wife, mother, mother-in-law, and mine to God brought him back to life."[99]

"Polina, at the age of more than 80 years old, had died twice over the course of three years, but with the ardent plea of her son and daughter Heaven brought her back." "Relatives don't want to part with their dearest ones. To some, maybe, coming back will bring sufferings, if earthly lessons are finished. And there are many such cases when relatives ask me to bring back to life their family members. God brings back to life, not me. I only ask, pray, read, as I already wrote, and say 150 times a daily prayer 'Song to Holy Mother of God.' God and Heaven are one for all religions, and He decides to whom He will prolong life if the soul didn't cross the middle of the so-called bridge. It is possible with God's will to return it back into the body, back to life. If the soul crossed the middle of the bridge, and felt the sweetness of Paradise, it doesn't want to come back, here it is already in God's hands, He will decide everything."[100]

In the described cases here, "these people wanted very much to live, they didn't cross the middle of the bridge, and Heaven prolonged life to them. They probably deserved it."[101]

Once the sessions with Tatiana come to a conclu-

Tatiana lighting candles as she prays for clients in a Russian Orthodox church

---

99. Sibirskaya, Tatiana, *Miracles and Mysteries of God*, 2005, 5.
100. Sibirskaya, Tatiana, *Miracles and Mysteries of God*, 2005, 5–6.
101. Sibirskaya, Tatiana, *Miracles and Mysteries of God*, 2005, 6.

sion, she continues to pray for her clients and often lights candles at church for them. "I am often tired from the energy drained from my body from so much prayer, but God has always restored and renewed my power, sometimes even stronger than before."[102] Her devotion to God, her clients, the earth, and all of mankind is truly extraordinary.

Tatiana's advice to people is to "always think positive. This gives a positive effect and also has an important meaning for recovery. Negative thoughts give negative effects. Negative people and negative thoughts are not open to God, and people with this outlook have trouble with their job, their friends, their family and their health."[103] "For in God's eyes we are all equal, whether we are rich, famous, or poor. He loves us all for who we are. So, I live and work in Brooklyn, and every day miraculous recoveries happen."[104]

---

102. Sibirskaya, Tatiana, Newsletter, Volume 1, Issue 1, October 1, 2004.
103. Sibirskaya, Tatiana, *Autobiography of a Faith Healer*, 2004, 19.
104. Sibirskaya, Tatiana, *Autobiography of a Faith Healer*, 2004, 21.

TESTIMONIALS

Over the course of my children's lives, Tatiana has helped my family immensely. With God's help, she has healed broken bones, concussions and asthma. She has also cured massive headaches, pneumonia and bronchitis, and eradicated Lyme disease. Currently she is helping my eighty-two-year-old mother who has Alzheimer's, and my eighty-seven-year-old father who collapsed from heart problems while caring for my mother. My mother is now much more lucid, and the doctors couldn't find any further evidence of my father's heart deterioration as he continues to care for my mother, rake leaves and shovel snow. As significant as all these miracles have been, I am most grateful for her prayers in saving my sons' lives. Depression has filled one son's mind with thoughts of suicide, and her constant prayers have lifted his spirits, filling him with God's light. God also saved my other son and a close friend from death in a tragic car accident, while Tatiana kept them in her healing prayers. She continues to pray for all of us, watching over us on a daily basis. We would not be here if it hadn't been for Tatiana's prayers and God's miracles. I thank God for his love and protection, and Tatiana for being such an important part of our lives. Despite dealing with many challenges, we know that we are truly blessed. (C. D. December 2015)

I met Tatiana in July 2010. We have had numerous sessions together. She is a clairvoyant channel of God's energy, and I can see and feel the energy coming from her. During our sessions, a very bright light opens on my crown chakra, and I feel very still and warm and happy. I can feel the energy moving around and concentrating on my body parts—in those areas that Tatiana mentioned had problems. Specifically, I had a thyroid lump that has almost disappeared, ovarian cysts that reduced significantly in size [proven by repeat pre and post ultrasound], and she healed glaucoma in my left eye—I no longer have pain or difficulty in my left eye. She is gentle and pleasant and loving and reassuring. It is an honor to be in her energy. She has changed my life and because of her, I now pray and go to church. Thank you Tatiana. I love you. (G. September 29, 2010)

I am very grateful for the help I received through Tatiana. I am thankful for her prayers and her concern for my wellbeing. I came to her with several health problems. Now I feel much better. The doctor informed me that my cholesterol showed great improvement; my sinuses have improved. Overall, I feel good. Thank you, Tatiana, and God bless you. (A. W. February 13, 2009)

I asked God to help me get rid of all my physical ailments so I can properly devote myself to my spiritual practice. A few days later, Tatiana showed up in my life. She correctly diagnosed all the symptoms I was suffering from and with God's permission she healed them. I know deep down inside that something changed in my body. I feel younger and healthier. During her sessions, I felt the warm energy working on the body parts that needed it. Having met Tanya made a big difference in my life. She is such a kind devoted lady. (R. A. April 8, 2009)

I would like to give my most heartfelt thanks to you for bringing this miraculous healing power to me. I asked God to heal me and Tanya came into my life as a messenger of divine intervention. Now, my body is healing and becoming stronger again and more balanced. I appreciate this love and light brought into my life and know it to have changed something in me forever. (M. R. April 8, 2009)

Dear Tatiana. It has been a great gift to meet you and I would like to sincerely thank you for your remarkable healing prayers. Your love, compassion, and pure dedication to serving God and selflessly helping as many as possible on this earth is an inspiration and example to all of us.

The energy and presence of God's healing force in each of the ten prayer sessions has been a very powerful experience, working on many levels beyond the physical. Thank you for helping to clear and strengthen my body, eliminate my headaches, and especially for helping to remove the pressure and discomfort in my eyes, which allowed me to return to a regular work schedule on the computer more quickly.

I also noticed an increased sense of calm and optimism throughout the week, and a greater lightness of being. It is a true joy to know that you are here, and making such a difference in the lives of those who have found their way to you.

Wishing you many, many blessings.

With many thanks,
A. (June 5, 2008)

I want to express sincere gratitude to Tanya for her noble and titanic work, for helping me to get rid of high blood pressure and my husband of kidney problems. God Bless you! We wish you many more wonderful experiences in your work.

Believe it or not? It is for you, the reader to decide.

Thank you so much, Saint Tanya. (O. M. June 5, 2008)

Tanya, God's love is flowing within every cell of your body. Your sweet moments of meditation, your nurturing, and the awareness of God's love within you, healing is the natural result. Your healing energy is providing me a renewal of mind and body. I feel refreshed and energized. May God bless you, and I wish you all the best in your future. (J. A. June 2, 2008)

I brought my mother to Tatyana after a series of very traumatic falls which resulted in a collarbone fractured in three places and a dislocated shoulder. The last fall resulted in her arm being ripped from the shoulder socket and her ring finger being fractured. We took her to the emergency room, and after much testing, they concluded that she was medically unstable to perform a surgery to repair all of this. Her insulin level was 456, sodium 150 below normal, and her white blood cell count was elevated. To make matters worse, she had heart dysrhythmia. Leaving her in the hospital was out of the question as she also suffers from Alzheimer's. She would most likely need to be restrained in order to carry out any sort of treatment in such threatening surroundings. I find this to be a personally unacceptable fate for my mother or any other person I love. People need to have a deep desire to live in order to heal and my mother wanted to die. She was 89 lbs. soaking wet and down to a piece of bread and lots of water or milky tea throughout the day. There had to be divine intervention, and although I can heal others, healing my mother was too dangerous, so I came to the best healer and dearest friend I know. My mother did not want to accept treatment initially and had to be coerced. My family was against it other than my father who has been helped by Tatyana before. Things did get progressively worse to all appearances before a shift occurred, and my mom started to eat. First out of curiosity to keep her company I brought all her favorite foods to eat while visiting her. She asked to try. I obliged. She then began to accept food from my father then began to demand food. Slowly her mind began to become clearer for longer periods. She began to remember little things like my son's age after two to three days. She began to express joy at seeing me. This, to me, is the greatest accomplishment as my mom has shown no real emotion towards me in years. Her arm turned from all black to almost white. She is slowly able to use her hand although her shoulder is still immobile and a source of pain. She notices little things about people and can hold a conversation that shows thought and discernment. The memory lapses are still present but not constant. She is expressing an interest in her appearance. She is able to pick her arm up to almost shoulder height and can get dressed on her own. (M. P. February 25, 2006)

Dear Tatiyana, thank you for your prayers. I feel better than when I started. I will continue to pray and hope that you will do the same. I believe that through God, all things are possible and He will strengthen me. Again, thank you. (R. A. July 11, 2005)

Dear Tatyana,

It is with love and gratitude that I write this letter of testimony for my healing sessions with you from June through November 2004.

On Thursday, June 3, I was celebrating my sixtieth birthday in the East Village, NYC, and happened to pass by a health food store where I picked up a copy of the Yoga Expo program starting the following Friday evening, June 4. On the train ride home, I read it and came across your ad. I was in an exhausted and debilitated state, but I knew I had to push myself to see you.

At the lecture that Friday, you diagnosed me correctly and beyond what I already knew or would tell anyone. I mentioned a hearing loss in my left ear, and you immediately offered the reason. I left your workshop that evening on a high vibrational level. The next morning, hearing improved in my left ear. Upon taking a shower, I noticed a beet-red section an inch wide along a five-inch length scar from a surgical procedure performed about thirty-five years ago. I knew it was toxic release and experienced relief. The normal skin color soon returned. The following Monday, I proceeded to end negative relationships. I was traveling and encased in divine energies. There was no question in my heart and soul that I would open my whole being to your healing work.

It was always so beautiful to be in your presence—for you are a master of healing exuding the wondrous gold energies of our Lord and His Servants. You were so gentle and kind in your words and most generous in all that you had to give. I shall never forget you and the love that streamed into the room during our sessions. I cry with joy and happiness as I write this letter and stop for a while to compose myself.

In the beginning of our sessions, I needed to rest more and realized a detoxification process was going on. After the second session, I had pains in my abdominal and intestinal areas at work, went home, doubled over in excruciating pain, and called out to you. I then remembered what you told me to do if I went into pain. Within a matter of minutes, I drifted off to sleep. The next day, I was so weak, I could not get up to go to work. When I saw you the following Saturday you said, 'It is working.' I would regularly check and examine my body knowing that all was improving.

Tatyana, my life continuously changed as I met with you. I can hear in my left ear and no longer have stomach and intestinal pains. I also know that all my bodies—physical, emotional, mental and spiritual—are stronger and healthier. Your energies catapulted me to even higher energies and are helping me daily to make wiser and more loving choices.

My blessings unto you,
W. Z. (December 6, 2004)

Dear lady Tanya, you have been helping me all my life, when I was sick with those diseases, or when I was sad or depressed. You were always a friend that would listen and understand. Also, you give great advice and explain your secrets [to those who live a lot of lives and those who lived little]. You take the time to talk to our Lord, our almighty here by the name of God, you also go back into my old lives and tell me about them. You don't just do it just for me, you do it for everybody! You talk to the angels because you are one! May God always keep his eye on you! Your friend, S. S. (May 6, 2004)

Thank you, Tanya, for the healing and the hope. I am emotionally, mentally and spiritually healthier, and I have faith in my physical health and abundance. I could feel the energy moving during the sessions, and feel the difference afterward. I am very appreciative that I found Tanya and had the gift of healing. H. L. (September 24, 2004)

Dear Tanya, having undergone my many healing sessions with you over the last two months, the sessions have now come to a completion. I want to thank you for being a vessel, channeling God's energy through you to me to heal my body.

You have been blessed with a miraculous gift from God to share with the people. I have been very fortunate to have been guided to you to receive this gift of love and healing energy. You are a selfless and wonderful loving soul who gives of herself to helping people who are suffering from illnesses and pain.

With God's love and energy, all is possible. I thank God and I thank you for all your efforts to relieve me of my discomforts.

Eternally grateful. With love, N. P. (July 10, 2004)

Tanya is amazing. She helped me out so much. I am really happy that we found her. I only wish that we found her sooner. She is a one of a kind doctor that makes you feel better. She is the best. (F. May 26, 2004)

TATIANA SIBIRSKAYA: A LIFE DEVOTED TO PERFORMING GOD'S MIRACLES

Dear Tanya, when I go to you and rest for forty-five minutes you heal both my insides and my outsides. Tanya after all ten sessions with you I feel great! After all, Tanya, God bless you! Love, D. (July 12, 2004)

I am E. G. of Miami Beach, Florida. I read about Tatyana during the Life Expo in New York City in March 2003. At that time, I had so much arthritic pain in my right knee, I was virtually crippled, but after each session with Tatyana, I improved remarkably. She projected ten sessions, and truthfully by the ninth, I was moving about, up/down stairs on the subway, and walking ten to twenty blocks with great ease and confidence. She claims to be a faith healer, but I know that it is purely scientific how she projects energy for realigning the body, because all the praying I ever did never healed my knee and life like Tatyana Sibirskaya! (E. G. April 11, 2003)

Dear Tatiana, thank you and God bless you for making me feel alive and with so much energy. Thank you and the angels for removing my allergies and hay fever, for opening my heart and giving such love. You are truly God's gift. As you bless us, we bless you as well.

Long life and good health, so that you may continue God's work. I thank the angels, I thank God, and I thank you.

All my love, P. W. (March 20, 2003)

A gift from God. One's life is a gift from God. One's life is something one should cherish and be thankful for. It is something one should never take for granted.

Although today I am healthy, I wasn't always this way. There were times when I was younger when I was very ill. I remember I couldn't breathe. I remember waking up in the night and asking to go outside because I felt as though there wasn't enough air in the lungs. I felt as though I was going to asphyxiate to death. My parents took me to the doctor who told them to take me to the hospital. I didn't want to go to the hospital for I felt as though it would be a terrifying experience. Listening to my pleading cries, they decided to call Tatiana. She asked to talk to me on the phone. Immediately as soon as I heard her voice, I began to feel a great amount of oxygen filling my lungs; and then within the ten minutes, I had spent talking on the phone I began to breathe like my normal self. Ever since that day, I had never doubted the fact that Tatiana is truly blessed with a gift from God. She has the power to cure many illnesses. I would like to thank Tatiana for helping me through times both thick and thin (times I was sick and not feeling well), but I know that she will say that it isn't her who saves the lives of people but God and so I thank Him as well. (C. Age 15, June 26, 2003)

To whom it may concern:

Tatyana helped me very much with the way I felt. I was not well in my being and through prayer now I feel alive again. She also prayed for my mother who has MS, and I have seen good results from this. Thank you, Tatyanna, for everything you have done for me and given me. I will never forget you and I love you. Thanks.

God bless and be with you always. A.H.

P.S. May God always dwell in your heart and soul! (January 28, 2003)

Dear Tatyana, when I first learned about you, I was surprised that there are people in this world, like you, that can perform the miracles you perform and be so happy and positive, when almost everyone around you is sick or overwhelmed with the problems and struggles they have to face in their lives.

I am glad there are some people in this world like you, Tanya. You give us strength and courage; you help us find happiness even when things aren't going our way, and you help strengthen our beliefs in God the Almighty, while you heal us with him by your side.

I am grateful to have met you and to have seen you perform miracles in my life. I hope you are forever prosperous, happy, and glad to do the massive job you do, which is helping people around the globe to live better lives.

Thank you, and God bless you, Tanya. Love forever, I. Y. (June 11, 2002)

Flowers from grateful clients

Thank you Tania for your help. If it wasn't for your prayers maybe I will not be in this world today. Thanks again. —E. T. (May 7, 2002)

"Eight years ago, I was diagnosed with breast cancer at the age of forty. I underwent a mastectomy and breast reconstruction, followed by six months of chemotherapy. The chemotherapy pushed me into an early menopause, and for the next six years, I was plagued with severe menopausal symptoms including hot flashes, headaches, breast pain, hemorrhaging, insomnia, fatigue, and depression. I could not take hormones because of the cancer risk. Most of the time, I did not feel well, and almost all of the time, I lived in fear of a recurrence of cancer.

In May of 1995, I was introduced to Tatiana. Without any prior knowledge of my condition, Tatiana was able to tell that I had had breast cancer, surgery, and intravenous chemotherapy and correctly described a full range of my symptoms. After meeting Tatiana, I began to feel better, and within a few weeks, my symptoms disappeared. From my personal point of view, there are many factors that might account for this, but what Tatiana provided to me was less of a physiological nature than a spiritual nature. Knowing her has strengthened my religious beliefs and has made me more aware of my own spiritual side. Apart from the relief of my physical problems, I have become more philosophical—and the debilitating fear of cancer that I lived with for such a long time is no longer there. (B. K. 1997)

To whom it may concern:

In September 1991, in the newspaper, we read about the clairvoyant and healer Tatiana Sibirskaya who came to Israel for a visit. My husband and I got an appointment to see Tatiana Sibirskaya the first day she was receiving patients. We immediately believed in the power of this pleasant and kind woman. She was radiating kindness and love. Ms. Sibirskaya explained to us that her healing is based on faith in God, and it is his energy that helps her to diagnose patients, determine a number of sessions for them, and cure the patients.

After a course of treatment with Tatiana, my husband and I were able to get rid of the spine pains. Tatiana removed an implant from the heart valve which blocked my blood circulation and caused me a lot of trouble.

My husband and I are immensely grateful to Ms. Tatiana Sibirskaya.

Sincerely yours, I. and L. L."
(September 3, 1997)

Dearest Tanya, there are not enough words for your love and prayers. You are a wonderful gifted person. With all my pain and illness I have suffered for many years, talking with you has relieved me of my agony. Matter of fact, I would not of been able to write this myself a month ago. My hands were in such pain I couldn't hold a pen. May God be with you. You and God gave me my life back. My doctors told me in April 2012 that I wouldn't live till July. I Love You. (J.)

I thank God to put me in contact with Tatyana. For many years, I was looking for a person with strong faith in God to help me. I was always debilitating with malaise and illness without names. The medical field could not help me. So far I could not find answer with the alternative medicine. I visited Tatyana's office every day for two weeks, and I feel great comfort and hope. I believe that in time and continued prayers I will solve my medical problems and also have control of my entire life. Blessed be God. Praise to Tatyana. Keep doing the Lord's work. You are one of the chosen few. (G.)

To Tatiana. Words cannot express all that you have done for me. You are an angel and a gift from God, and I am so blessed to have met you. I will never forget you and will always smile when I think of you and all of God's work you are doing here on Earth. You have changed my life and helped me find myself again and this is the greatest gift you can give anyone so I thank you sincerely with all my being. You have given me hope again and reminded me of God's love for me and how to connect to it again.

You were a gift from God to me and I will thank you and love you always.

Eternally with love, V.

Dear Tanya,

This is to express my deep respect and gratitude for your meaningful, tireless, world class, lifelong efforts toward helping people on their last hope. You remarkably helped me overcome obstacles on my life journey and brought back joy of life and a better understanding for all and everything. Most importantly, you brought to the fore that the impossible is possible, if we truly believe in it and never give up!

I would like to thank you for your sincere, outstanding, and illuminating work that changed everything and ultimately brought me closer to the supreme!

With love, D.

Dear Tanya, thank you so much for helping me find health and energy again. The scar on my face has healed beautifully and my cysts in my breast are gone too! I feel God's energy and thank you and God for allowing me to be blessed enough to find you. I am truly blessed to know you and your work.

Much love, M.

Dear Tatiana,

I am very thankful for everything you have done for me. Ever since I have known you, you have helped me with my health problems. I had big problems with my legs, and you helped me. When I was depressed, you helped me again. You made me feel wonderful again. You also help healing my children when they had been sick. Thank you so much for everything. And thank you so much to God for making it happen. I would also like to thank God making it possible for me to get to know you.

Thank you, Tatiana. God bless you. Love, C.

Just wanted to say thank you. I would not be on this trip with my mother and husband without your help. I think of you often. God bless. —M.

QUESTIONS AND ANSWERS

Q: Can anyone learn to do what you do?
A: "No, never. What I have is God's gift. I can use it only to do good to people."[105] "The cure comes from God. The success depends not upon the kind of disease, but upon the person himself: what kind of a man he is, how many good things he has done in his life. God sends diseases to man and the cure of these diseases is also in His hands."[106]

Q: How many sessions do most people need?
A: "There is no rule here. It is very individual. Some need just one, for some 12 is not enough. The goal is to cure the patient."[107]

Q: Does one have to be religious to be healed?
A: "Much depends on their faith. Sometimes those who don't believe start believing, those who do become more confident in their faith. But my patients are people of different religions,

---

105. Grant, Alexander, *Tatiana Sibirskaya—the Messenger of God's Will*, "Novoye Russkoe Slovo," "New Russian Word," April 4, 1997, 2.
106. Grant, Alexander, *Tatiana Sibirskaya—the Messenger of God's Will*, "Novoye Russkoe Slovo," "New Russian Word," April 4, 1997, 3.
107. Lishak, Arnold, *I Am Happy to Bring Happiness to People*, Interview with Tatiana Sibirskaya, "Mir," October 2-8, 1992.

TATIANA SIBIRSKAYA: A LIFE DEVOTED TO PERFORMING GOD'S MIRACLES

nations and races."[108] "I heal people, not parishioners."[109] "There is only one God, and we all, healthy and sick, righteous and sinners, are his children."[110]

Q: You are not a doctor. How can you diagnose?

A: "I tell my patients what I have to tell. Sometimes it seems to me as if I am reading it from a list. If a patient has problems with liver, I explain to him what is wrong. Neither he nor I need special terminology to understand that. The most important thing for both of us is the process of treatment and the result. The cure of both the mind and the body."[111]

Q: Have you had patients with cancer?

A: "Yes. At the early stage of the disease it is not a problem at all, but at a later stage with metastases the treatment is much more complicated, though the people were cured even in these cases."[112]

Q: Are there ever patients that you cannot help?

A: "During the first six years of practicing it has happened just twice. I felt that I would be incapable to help them. It was too late. My heart broke."[113]

Q: What do you see when you contact God?

A: "It is like a cloud, something light and pure, and images of Saints...and God. How does he look like? I do not know.

---

108. Grant, Alexander, *Tatiana Sibirskaya—the Messenger of God's Will*, "Novoye Russkoe Slovo," "New Russian Word," April 4, 1997.
109. Hurgin, Boris, *Bow to Tatiana with Gratitude*, "Novoye Russkoe Slovo," "New Russian Word," April 19, 1994.
110. Hurgin, Boris, *Bow to Tatiana with Gratitude*, "Novoye Russkoe Slovo," "New Russian Word," April 19, 1994.
111. Grant, Alexander, *Tatiana Sibirskaya—the Messenger of God's Will*, "Novoye Russkoe Slovo," "New Russian Word," April 4, 1997.
112. Hurgin, Boris, *Bow to Tatiana with Gratitude*, "Novoye Russkoe Slovo," "New Russian Word," April 19, 1994.
113. Gris, Henry, *And So Tatiana Sibirskaya Became the World's Latest Healer*, International Artists Guild, Ltd. Matthew, Inc., Nov.17, 1992, 7.

Something overwhelming and shiny, without any form or shape, God's grace, warmth…it is unique for every man."[114]

Q: Does the devil exist?
A: "Yes, evil force, something dark. It can cure your body, but takes your soul. It gives a man temporary relief of the pain. There is no real cure, because soul remains dark. All bad and evil burns in the light of a candle."[115]
Q: Do you only work on people in New York?
A: "No, not only here. I work on people all around the world."[116]
Q: How do you feel about modern medicine?
A: "Medicine does a lot of good to people. However, I also treat many doctors. They are always afraid to admit incapability of medical science to find the cure in some cases and their forced necessity to look for help somewhere else. Some of them come incognito. They don't want to be seen by anybody. It takes courage to admit that a medical specialist with scientific knowledge asks for help from a clairvoyant."[117]
Q: What about homeopathy?
A: "I believe it is from God too. God created herbs, as everything on this earth. That means it is for our good, to help us."[118]
Q: Are there other people around the world who are like you?
A: "Yes, there are 12 of us. Unfortunately I don't know much about them and their work."
Q: Twelve, as in the twelve apostles?

---

114. Hurgin, Boris, *Bow to Tatiana with Gratitude*, "Novoye Russkoe Slovo," "New Russian Word," April 19, 1994.
115. Hurgin, Boris, *Bow to Tatiana with Gratitude*, "Novoye Russkoe Slovo," "New Russian Word," April 19, 1994.
116. Hurgin, Boris, *Bow to Tatiana with Gratitude*, "Novoye Russkoe Slovo," "New Russian Word," April 19, 1994.
117. Hurgin, Boris, *Bow to Tatiana with Gratitude*, "Novoye Russkoe Slovo," "New Russian Word," April 19, 1994.
118. Hurgin, Boris, *Bow to Tatiana with Gratitude*, "Novoye Russkoe Slovo," "New Russian Word," April 19, 1994.

A: "Yes, I think so."[119]
Q: Can you treat all illnesses?
A: "Most of them."[120]
Q: Why is there so much suffering here on Earth?
A: "I asked Heaven why people basically suffer on Earth. The answer was: people withdraw from God, the chase after material values exceeds spiritual values. Everybody must reconsider his or her life, and then there will be Paradise on Earth."[121]
Q: Do you practice group therapy as well as private sessions?
A: "Yes, I also practice group therapy. Very few faith healers have mastered group therapy because of the difficulty in diagnosing and treating cancerous tumors in one patient, depression and bipolar disorder in another, and osteoporosis in yet a third…all at the same time! I often get tired from my work because I concentrate so hard, and I act as a medium to absorb the pains of my patients, so working in groups is more physically and mentally draining for me. But this is something that, with God's help, I have developed over the many years of my practice, both in Russia as well as in the United States. I also pray for groups of people in afflicted communities."[122]

---

119. Tatiana Sibirskaya in discussion with the author, December, 2015.
120. Lishak, Arnold, *I Am Happy to Bring Happiness to People*, Interview with Tatiana Sibirskaya, "Mir," October 2–8, 1992.
121. Sibirskaya, Tatiana, *Miracles and Mysteries of God*, 2005.
122. Sibirskaya, Tatiana, Newsletter, Volume 1, Issue 1, October 1, 2004.

BIBLIOGRAPHY

Basin, Yuri, *Ordinary Miracle*, "Yevreiski Mir," Jewish World, May 2, 1997 #4

Grant, Alexander, *Tatiana Sibirskaya—the Messenger of God's Will*, "Novoye Russkoe Slovo", "New Russian Word," April 4, 1997.

Gris, Henry, *And So Tatiana Sibirskaya Became the World's Latest Healer*, International Artists Guild, Ltd. Matthew, Inc., Nov.17, 1992.

Hurgin, Boris, *Bow to Tatiana with Gratitude*, "Novoye Russkoe Slovo," "New Russian Word," April 19, 1994.

Lishak, Arnold, *I Am Happy to Bring Happiness to People*, Interview with Tatiana Sibirskaya, "Mir", October 2–8, 1992.

Sibirskaya, Tatiana, *Autobiography of a Faith Healer*, 2004.

Sibirskaya, Tatiana, *Miracles and Mysteries of God*, 2005.

Sibirskaya, Tatiana, Newsletter, Volume 1, Issue 1, October 1, 2004.

Tatiana Sibirskaya in discussion with the author, December, 2015.

Viktorova, L., *I See Your Heart*, "Vecherniy Dushanbe," "Evening Dushanbe," October 2, 1991.

ABOUT THE AUTHOR

Always looking for creative outlets, Carolyn Fryer gravitated toward writing through the inspiration of her aging parents. Determined to write their life stories while they could still tell them, Carolyn first wrote about her father's life and travels. This book was followed by a book about her mother's ancestry, chronicling five generations of her family back to their Norwegian roots. Carolyn's third project was to tell her own life story about the experiences she had traveling around the world as a professional musician. Having shared these books with Tatiana Sibirskaya, Tatiana then asked Carolyn to write a biography about her. This book is the product of their collaboration.

Printed in the USA
CPSIA information can be obtained
at www.ICGtesting.com
LVHW072232010923
756937LV00026BA/545

9 781681 972725